Newbury

IN OLD PHOTOGRAPHS

PETER ALLEN

Alan Sutton Publishing Limited
Phoenix Mill · Far Thrupp · Stroud
Gloucestershire · GL5 2BU

First published 1995

Cover illustration: The Broadway, June 1928 (see p. 15).

British Library Cataloguing in Publication Data.
A catalogue record for this book is available from the British Library.

ISBN 0-7509-0887-4

Typeset in 9/10 Sabon.
Typesetting and origination by
Alan Sutton Publishing Limited.
Printed in Great Britain by
Hartnolls, Bodmin, Cornwall.

Newbury Bridge, *c.* 1900.

Contents

An early view of Wharf Street (looking east), showing the Old Cloth Hall (centre), 1860s. This photograph is taken from one of a collection of lantern slides found under the floor of the old Lecture Hall at the Newbury United Reformed Church in 1989.

Introduction

Newbury in the nineties is a town that is changing fast. Until forty years ago it was a sedate market town, although even then there were omens of what was to come. As a national crossroads (the A4 runs east to west and the A34 north to south) the town centre was often congested with traffic, especially in high summer. At that time, however, Newbury probably meant little more to people travelling through than a passing inconvenience.

In keeping with national trends the rate of change quickened during the sixties, but in the early seventies the opening of the M4 took away much of the east–west traffic. Thereafter, Newbury was increasingly cited in the media as one of the hi-tech boom towns of 'Silicon Valley' (the M4 corridor). In the eighties, too, it became associated in the national consciousness with Greenham Common and cruise missiles.

These things are fading into history today, although echoes of the recent past persist. Modern road development has failed to keep pace with the rising tide of vehicles. In the nineties Newbury is still a bottle-neck, particularly on race days – motorists trying to get through the place must curse the congestion more heartily than did those of forty years ago.

Nevertheless, for those people to whom Newbury is 'home' – whether by birth or adoption – the town is far more than its passing image. Newbury's name may imply that it is a 'new borough' but it has a rich history. There is no need to repeat it in detail here, as a number of local history books are now available which do just that. Most of what they say can be traced back to the published researches of local historian Walter Money (1836–1926), whose *magnum opus*, *The History of the Ancient Town and Borough of Newbury*, was published in 1887. This 600-page work of reference dealt with the history of the place from Roman times through to the nineteenth century.

Suffice to say, Newbury as such is first mentioned in a document dated 1079 but the locality was inhabited long before this. Archaeological evidence indicates that the locality was occupied in the Stone Age, both in Palaeolithic times, at Wash Common, and Mesolithic times, at Greenham. There is also evidence of Roman life – and death – here, with – for example – the discovery of a Roman cemetery when the town's railway goods yard was being built in 1856. Evidence of Saxon settlement in Newbury is scarce but it is likely that here was 'Ulvritone', referred to in *Domesday Book*.

References to Newbury itself begin around the time of the Norman Conquest. A planned town probably developed on the south bank of the River Kennet – confirmed by excavations in the present Cheap Street/Bartholomew Street area preparatory to the building of the Kennet Centre in around 1980.

Development gradually spread to the area north of the river (now Northbrook Street, but for centuries better known as Speenhamland).

Tradition has it that there was once a castle in the town and that it was besieged by King Stephen in 1152, although no trace of it exists today. It is believed that in the early thirteenth century King John founded the town's hospital of St Bartholomew (now almshouses). A 'borough' by Edward I's reign, Newbury sent two burgesses to his parliament in 1275. In modern Northbrook Street a remnant of the house of Jack o' Newbury is testimony to the town's prosperity from the medieval cloth trade. John Winchcombe's real monument, however, is the parish church of St Nicolas, completed after his death, in around 1532.

In the seventeenth century Newbury witnessed two battles during the Civil War, one at Wash Common in 1643 and the other at Shaw-cum-Donnington in 1644. Shaw House (built by Thomas Dolman, another rich cloth merchant) was involved in the second battle, although Donnington Castle was more central to the action. In the eighteenth century the part of the town known as Speenhamland (around the modern clocktower) featured large in the coaching business; forty-two coaches a day passed through here. Then, during the nineteenth-century era of Victorian respectability, photography came of age.

The photographs included in this book start from that date and bring us up to the present day. I have assembled a variety of views of Newbury: from the ceremonial to the everyday, from the special to the mundane, from streets and buildings to people and places. In Newbury things change so quickly. For instance, memories of Northbrook Street before its recent traffic-calming measures and partial pedestrianization may soon fade.

Like many a town Newbury needs to have pictures of its past recorded for posterity. This is partly so that future generations will be able to study these images and see what went before; equally, it is so that the present generation of Newburians may peruse them and say 'I remember . . .'. I hope this book will go some way towards meeting these objectives.

Peter Allen, 1995

Street Scenes

Walter Money described Newbury's three main streets as 'placed somewhat in the form of the letter Y'. These are Cheap Street, the 'Chepe' or Market Street; Bartholomew Street, named after the ancient hospital; and Northbrook Street, so called from the brook which traverses its course northwards. This view of Northbrook Street (looking north) in the 1860s shows the town as Walter Money knew it. 'No one who is a lover of antiquity can fail to walk through Newbury without noticing its ancient gabled houses,' he wrote, 'too few, alas, but still a sufficient number are left to show us how quaint the old town must have looked.' One wonders what he would make of Newbury today.

A postcard view of Northbrook Street, the town's main thoroughfare, when the pace of life was more leisurely, around the turn of the century.

Market Place, showing the Town Hall and the statue of Queen Victoria which was once located here, *c.* 1904.

Market Place, looking north, *c.* 1904. This postcard features Queen Victoria's statue, erected as a memorial to the late monarch. It was made at the Royal Doulton Potteries, Lambeth, and was presented to the town in 1902. It was a gift from 'Lord' George Sanger, of circus fame. A local man, his father had kept a stall at Newbury market. The statue was unveiled by his daughter, Mrs Reeve, on Wednesday 24 June 1903. It stood 38 ft high and in the south-facing recess (seen here) was a female figure holding a wreath and representing 'fame'. To improve traffic flow in Market Place, the statue was moved to Greenham House gardens in 1933, and – minus two of its lions – to Victoria Park in 1966.

Cheap Street, looking north, *c.* 1908. The New Market Inn, adjacent to the cobbled entrance to Market Street (left), has since been demolished.

Oxford Street, looking north, *c.* 1908. In the fork of the Oxford and Bath roads at the top of the street the old toll-house (Wells' Bakery) can be seen.

Now you see it. . . . The Mansion House, which gave its name to the street, with the Shambles below, looking east, *c.* 1908. It was built by John Clarke in 1742.

Now you don't. . . . The Mansion House, looking west, *c.* 1909. Demolished to improve traffic flow here, the Municipal Offices were built in its place.

The view across Northbrook Street, from Jack Lane to Stradling and Plenty's Motor Works and Garage, *c.* 1913. The northern gable end is all that remains of Jack o' Newbury's fifteenth-century house.

The Broadway, *c.* 1914. The Jubilee Clock was unveiled by Mr George Knight, Mayor of Newbury, on 4 March 1889. The horse trough in front was supplied by the Metropolitan Drinking Fountain & Cattle Trough Association in 1908.

The Old Cloth Hall, 1928. Restored in memory of Queen Victoria, it opened in 1904 as the Museum of Antiquities and Curiosities.

The Jack Hotel at 22 Northbrook Street, *c*. 1913. This sometime coaching inn, named after Jack o' Newbury, was sold off in 1935 for redevelopment.

The Broadway, at the top of Northbrook Street, June 1928. The clocktower was erected as a memorial to half a century of Queen Victoria's reign (1887). In front is the Russian Gun, which was located here from 1889 until 1929, a relic of the Crimean War. On the island around the clocktower were four tall gas lamps and eight squat cast-iron bollards with chains. Only the clocktower remains today, and that was much modified in 1929.

Bartholomew Street, looking north, *c.* 1940. The imposing building on the left is the Regal Cinema. This opened in 1927, closed in 1962 and was demolished six years later.

The Broadway, looking east, *c.* 1940. The clocktower can be seen in its post-1929 form and behind it is the Flower House site, which has since been redeveloped.

Northbrook Street, with Liddiard's the butcher, on the left, looking north, June 1928. On the other side of the street are the premises of Milwards the shoe shop and Hughes the caterer, perhaps better known as the Bridge Restaurant. Further along on the right-hand side were the premises of the House of Toomer, an ironmongery business established in 1692. The neighbouring premises were occupied by Timothy White the chemists and Camp Hopson's drapery store.

Market Place, *c.* 1950. The Town Hall was rebuilt between 1878 and 1881. Its tall clocktower can still be seen and remains a landmark for miles around.

The Corn Exchange, *c.* 1950. Erected in 1861, it fell into disrepair over the years, but was restored for leisure use in 1993.

The old toll-house, at the junction of the Bath and Oxford roads north of the town centre, before its demolition in 1950. It ceased to be a toll-house in the nineteenth century, when it was purchased (in 1892) by William Wells and converted to Wells' Bakery. William ran the concern until his death in 1923; his wife continued the business until 1939, when the Council bought the property for road improvements. The building was demolished to widen the road at the junction and to give a better line of vision for motorists.

Bartholomew Street, looking north, *c.* 1964. Note that a two-way traffic system was then in force. The site of Nias Garage (formerly College House School, at the turn of the century) is now part of the Kennet Centre.

Northcroft Lane, looking west, *c.* 1964. The white building was the Rose & Crown pub. West Street joins the lane behind the woman with the pram.

Cheap Street, looking towards the old Sun pub, *c.* 1964. Beyond the pub was the entrance to the railway goods yard, before the new relief road was built.

West Street, looking west, *c.* 1964. Although the Lion pub still stands on the corner, this view has greatly changed since the Strawberry Hill development scheme.

Essex Street, at the southern end of the town, *c.* 1960. The street was named after the Earl of Essex, who led troops here in the first Battle of Newbury.

Postwar estate type housing in Elizabeth Avenue, named after Elizabeth II, *c.* 1960.

SECTION TWO
People and Places

Looking north up Oxford Street with the Chequers Hotel in the centre, *c.* 1950. Walter Money claimed that the Chequers was almost as well known in coaching days as the Pelican. It retains some original features but was rebuilt almost entirely when it was taken over by Trust Houses Ltd, for whom this photograph was taken.

A picnic group on Greenham Common, a popular leisure spot for Newbury folk around the turn of the century. From left to right: -?-, Miss Nora New, Miss ? Richards, Mrs J.H. Thompson, Miss Gertrude New, Mrs Ada New (mother of the two sisters), Mrs Kate Mortimer (in the bathchair), Mrs Tryphena Thompson, John Henry Thompson (see p. 32), with daughter Violet and son William. Mrs Mortimer ran a cake shop at 141 Bartholomew Street, serving from her bathchair with a long pair of tongs. Mr Thompson originated from Stroud, where he ran the local newspaper.

Methodism was brought to Newbury by John Wesley in around 1740 but the first Methodist chapel, in Northbrook Street, was not built until 1804. A new church was erected there in 1838. It was restored in 1898, around the time this photograph was taken. It shows members of the congregation at a garden party in the paddock of a house called Newlands, in Porchester Road. The group includes John Henry Thompson (back, left) with 'Bodger' Lewis in front of him and Charlie Griffin to his left. The girl with the big hat (front row) is Miss Nellie Bolton. Mr Thompson lived at a house named Axbridge in Howard Road but ran a pharmacy in Market Place; he was Mayor of Newbury in 1927.

George New (1840–98) with his wife Ellen and son Harry, in the garden of Brook House, 27 Bartholomew Street, *c.* 1890. The house has since been demolished.

Men of the Newbury troop of the Berkshire Yeomanry Cavalry, *c.* 1900. The group includes QM. Sgt. W. New (front, right) with Col. G. Ricardo (to his right).

Boys of Newbury's 1st Falkland Scouts outside a house in Andover Road, 1909. Bert Wheeler is to the left of the middle row and his brother Charlie is at the front, right.

Girls of Newbury's Salvation Army Drill Troupe outside the Salvation Army Hall in Northcroft Lane, 1911. The hall was inaugurated in 1883.

The paddock at Newbury racecourse, just before the First World War. The course was built at the instigation of a successful local trainer, John Porter. He was originally refused a licence to build a racecourse at Newbury, but a chance meeting with Edward VII resulted in royal support for the project. The stewards at the Jockey Club were persuaded to change their minds.

The grandstand at the racecourse, at around the same time. The first meeting was held at Newbury on 26 September 1905, attracting a crowd of fifteen thousand.

A unique postcard view showing the construction of the GWR station at the racecourse. It was opened for the first race meeting in September 1905.

In the days of steam, the locomotives of race specials from London were turned for their return journey on the racecourse station's turntable, as seen here, *c.* 1962.

Shaw House, *c.* 1906. Built for Thomas Dolman, this Tudor manor-house was a Royalist base in the second Battle of Newbury.

The memorial to Lord Falkland, who was killed here during the Civil War.

Remains of Donnington Castle, besieged and ruined during the Civil War.

The Old Cloth Hall was built in 1627, but within a hundred years, as the cloth trade declined, it was being used as a grain store instead. By the end of the nineteenth century, when this picture was taken, the building was in a state of decay.

W.G. New of Bartholomew Street as a young man, *c.* 1880.

Bert Elliott jnr as a member of the Royal Berkshire Regiment, *c.* 1914.

John Henry Thompson, Mayor of Newbury in 1927, with his wife.

The Chequers, *c.* 1950. Mr Pointer (left) and Mr Delahunty were hotel porters.

The men of Elliott's (furniture makers at the Albert Works) North Company Berkshire Home Guard, *c.* 1940. In peacetime Elliott's made furniture at the Albert Works, but during the war the company built aircraft.

The 38th Methodist Scouts outside Northbrook Street Methodist Church, *c.* 1934. The scoutmaster is Dick Drake (second row, centre).

St Nicolas' Church, with its stone gateway and the war memorial, 1928. It was Jack o' Newbury who 'built the church of Newberry' in around 1500.

The interior of the church, looking towards the altar, *c.* 1928. In the church there is a fine brass depicting Jack and his wife, Alice, with their children.

St John's Church before the First World War. Designed by William Butterfield, it was built of brick in the Decorated style and was consecrated in 1860.

The interior of the church, looking into the chancel, *c.* 1907. This church was destroyed in an air-raid in 1943 but a new church was erected in around 1955.

Journeymen and apprentices of the *Newbury Weekly News*, *c.* 1890. The men in bowler hats are overseers; Alfie Collins (right) served for seventy-two years.

Employees of the *NWN* on a 'wayzgoose', *c.* 1930. By that time packed lunches had replaced the roast goose treat of earlier company outings.

Printing the *NWN*, *c*. 1949. This Cossar machine was installed in 1936 and printed sixteen pages at the rate of four thousand per hour.

Typesetting the *NWN* by the old hot metal process at the Northbrook Street printworks. The works were superseded by the Faraday Road works in 1982.

Greenham Park, *c.* 1950. Here, in what was formerly the garden of Greenham House, Queen Victoria's statue was sited from 1933 to 1966.

Victoria Park, *c.* 1950. Once called The Marsh, it was renamed in 1901 in memory of the late monarch.

SECTION THREE
Special Occasions

In the nineteenth century the town's detachment of Royal Berkshire Yeomanry Cavalry was often recruited to help celebrate special events. A volunteer cavalry corps was first raised in Newbury in 1797 and eventually became part of the RBYC, with headquarters in Reading. This photograph shows the RBYC, under the command of QM. Sgt. W. New, on 22 June 1897, as part of the town's parade for Queen Victoria's diamond jubilee. The sight of the RBYC, '. . . in their scarlet uniforms and waving plumes, mounted on prancing chargers, was a good start, giving the procession quite an imposing appearance'. Here, they are passing shops on the west side of Northbrook Street.

(Above and opposite) Newbury photographer F.H. Rolfe recorded the laying of the foundation stone of the town's new 'free' library. The idea of a public library in Newbury had been proposed twenty years earlier, but it became a reality after Andrew Carnegie, the American philanthropist, gave the project £2,000. The picture shows local dignitaries at the foundation ceremony, including Newbury's mayor, Mr Frederick Hopson. The flags served to screen the dignitaries from the populace gathered behind them in Cheap Street, and the umbrellas were to protect them from the heat of the sun on this summer's day.

The foundation stone was lowered into place by Mrs Eleanor Palmer (wife of Mr George Palmer MP), of Marlston House, Hermitage, on Wednesday 28 June 1905. Beneath it were placed articles such as copies of the *Newbury Weekly News* and *The Times*, picture postcards of the town, coins of the realm and a copy of Walter Money's *Popular History of Newbury*, published that year. The library was built by Hoskings Brothers and opened in 1906. The first librarian was Mr J.W. Rosling, who handed books to borrowers after they chose them from a printed list. He was secretary of the town's Education Committee and censored those books he disapproved of.

Market Place, looking south, on Boxing Day, 1946. This is the venue for the start of the annual meet of the Vine and Craven Hunt.

Tank Day in Market Place, 30 May 1918. The tank toured Newbury and then spent the day here, promoting a campaign for the sale of war bonds.

A somewhat enigmatic photograph, whose caption states: 'Lord Roberts riding in car.' The picture was clearly taken in Market Place, outside The Old Waggon & Horses Inn, early this century. Lord Roberts was then a national celebrity, '. . . the darling of the public and the hero of Kandahar and of the Boer War'. In the years before the First World War, he was active in the Irish Home Rule issue, campaigning for the Unionist cause, and may have been driven here by chauffeur for that purpose. The car appears to be an 8 hp Napier of about 1899.

Northbrook Street, looking north, May 1935. The street, like others in Newbury, was decorated to celebrate the silver jubilee of George V.

Marking the jubilee at Wash Common: these families planted an oak tree, grown from an acorn, on a plot of ground there. The site is now 14 Battery End.

Another occasion to celebrate: VE Day, 8 May 1945. Like many others in Newbury, residents of Gloucester Road organized a street party. The photograph includes Mrs Kitchener (extreme right), Miss Diane Kitchener and Miss Pat Fraser.

On VE night people danced in the streets, but at daytime events, like this one in Gloucester Road, umbrellas and raincoats were kept to hand.

The Festival of Britain was held in the summer of 1951, and communities across the country joined in. In Newbury there was a fortnight of festivity, ending with a carnival on Saturday 23 June. A crowd of 35,000 people lined the streets to watch a 1½ mile procession with 1,000 people in over 450 tableaux presented on vehicles. The characters in front of this float include Mary Wyatt (as Bo-peep), Daphne Barnes (as a mandarin), June Pope (as a cowgirl) and Betty Preston (front, right). They are near the start of the procession, which began in Enborne Road, went round the town and finished at Stroud Green.

Newbury's 44th Remembrance Day ceremony on Sunday 11 November 1962. On brass panels, the town's war memorial records the names of almost three hundred Newburians, including civilian and Civil Defence personnel, who lost their lives in the wars. Here, Newbury's rector, the Revd G.C. Matthews, conducted a short service and the lesson was read by the Revd H.G. Davis, Congregational minister. Prayers were led by the Revd B.C. Foulger, of St John's, and Mr Jack Olive spoke the exhortation. Afterwards the mayor and Corporation, and various organizations, attended the morning service at the parish church.

Newbury's annual carnival remains an enjoyable tradition in the town. In 1968 it was held on 7 September and thousands turned out for it. Crowds seven-deep lined the route and traffic was diverted from the town centre as the procession made its way round the streets. The floats were judged by the town's mayor, Mr L.L. Hall, and recorder, Edward Terrell QC. This photograph shows the public library's entry, depicting 'Home Rule for Wessex', with only Alfred's burnt cakes for sustenance on the way round! In the evening over two hundred people attended the carnival dance at the Plaza.

School Days

Newbury's oldest school, St Bartholomew's, was founded in the sixteenth century as part of a charitable foundation. In the nineteenth century the town was served by a variety of private schools and others established by the National and British Schools Societies. During the twentieth century local authority schools assumed an increasingly dominant role in education. This photograph was taken in the hall at Speenhamland Church of England School, where the children are celebrating the coronation of George VI in 1937. The VIPs (centre) include the Mayor and Mayoress of Newbury, Mr and Mrs Clifford; between them is Mr J.W. Rosling. Left of the mayoress is Mr Lawrence (headmaster); his wife (a teacher) is standing by the Union Jack. The boy in front of the mayoress is Gerald Peck, while the girls include Joy Sanders, Georgina Spanswick, Elsie Smith, Mary Tidbury, Ivy Martin, Audrey Morris and Bertha Owen.

Speenhamland C. of E. School was built in 1835 and enlarged in 1880 and 1894. Class V is seen here in 1932, with teacher Miss Morgan.

Class IV at the same school in 1932, with teacher Mrs Lawrence. Pupils include Connie Drew, Barbara Gough, Sylvia Wiltshire and Jean Sumter.

St John's C. of E. School, Newtown Road, was built in 1874. These are the pupils of class 1a, including Peter Sanders (back row, third from right), *c.* 1931.

The 'new' Council School in Station Road, *c.* 1914. Opened on 10 March 1909, it was destroyed by wartime bombing on 10 February 1943.

A very early photograph of a class inside the Council School, *c*. 1912. It was quite a large school, built to accommodate 312 boys and 352 girls.

Class II of the Council School's Infant Department, with teacher Mrs Allen, 1928. Connie Drew is in the front row, second from left.

A class of older children at the Council School in about 1931, with teacher Miss Morgan, who presumably moved soon afterwards to Speenhamland (see p. 50).

Girls of class I at the Council School, with teacher Miss Eggleton, *c.* 1934. The pupils include Doreen Baldwin, Barbara Hill and Frances Blackford.

The back of College House School, a private school then operating at Herborough House, Bartholomew Street, *c.* 1900.

The interior of the school. It was run by a Miss Pollard, who lived on the premises. Could it be her reflection in the mirror?

The pupils and staff of St Bartholomew's Preparatory School in Enborne Road, *c.* 1937. Back row, left to right: Malcolm Fraser, 'Titch' Taylor, Peter Goddard, Peter Besant, Billy Qualington, John Payne, Rupert Wallis, Peter Hill, Charlie Eady, Ian Muir, Tony Boyer, Peter Rodbourne. Second row: Peter Wood, George Woolmer, David Gregory, Billy Bloxham, Jock Greenshields, Peter Thomas, John Harris, Colin Wadham, Bob Brown, Norman Metcalfe, Ian Hastie, David Able, Ivor Scull. Third row: Roger Game, Robin Wilson, Michael Turner, Mr L. Connell-Smith, Mr Donald Florey (headmaster), Miss M. Ward, Terry Langdon, John Patterson, Michael Davis. Front row: Stuart Drury, David Hopson, Nigel Fenner, Robert Harris, R. Colquoon, Peter Norman, Ben Pratt, Ross Caldicott, Ivor Gore, Billie Renshaw, David Pobjoy, John Wakeford.

St Bartholomew's Boys' Grammar School moved to this Enborne Road site in 1886. By 1930 the school catered for 213 boys (including 23 boarders).

The County Girls' High School opened in Andover Road in 1910 and catered for 200 girls, under the distinguished headteacher Miss E.J. Luker.

Shopping Days

Until quite recently Newbury's shops were family businesses in which the proprietors lived over the shop. The produce for sale was often home-grown or home-made and customers got personal service in shops specializing in particular products. Then, in 1929, Woolworths arrived in Newbury, followed by Marks and Spencer in 1935, beginning a trend in self-service stores which has continued to the present day. Newbury's market actually originated in medieval times. Market Place is seen here in 1866, at which date the Corn Exchange (where grain merchants and others set out their stalls) had only been open a few years. Buyers and sellers came into the town from miles around.

Ham Mill, on the eastern edge of the town, early this century. Here, New Brothers, millers and corn merchants, made products for sale at their town-centre shop.

W.G. New (left) in the doorway of his shop at 27 Bartholomew Street, at which he sold corn, cattle cake and poultry meal.

A fascinating photograph of the shop front of the Reading Industrial Co-operative Society at 38 Cheap Street, *c.* 1902. The Reading society had six shops in that town and branches elsewhere in the county; Newbury's was 'number four'. Its window displays advertise mild cured bacon, cheese and Cadbury's Cocoa. Provisions were delivered locally by roundsman John Wheeler (second from right), who is shown here with a small group of shop assistants. For at least the first quarter of this century the shop manager was Henry Charles Commerford. The shop was demolished in about 1961, when Bear Lane was widened.

The International Tea Company Stores at 4–8 Bartholomew Street, *c.* 1912. The shop assistants include Miss Dora Robey (seventh from left).

The premises of Ernest Kimber, grocery, wine and spirit merchant, at the corner of Bartholomew and Pound Streets, *c.* 1915. A delivery cart stands outside.

A splendid photograph of the shop front of Drews, market gardeners, at 98 Northbrook Street, *c.* 1930. The window display advertises the fact that the produce on sale was 'all grown on our own farm'. John Thomas Drew came to Newbury from Kent, where he had been a farmer, in 1928. He started Enborne Nurseries, and was known locally as a nurseryman and seedsman. He and his three sons grew produce to sell in the shop. The family traded here, and lived above the shop, until the last son retired from the business. The premises are now an optician's.

Vincent & Co., ironmongers, at 54–6 Bartholomew Street, *c.* 1930. Still an ironmonger's, the shop is now owned by House of Toomer.

The premises of Joseph Higgs, pork butcher and bacon curer, at 25 Bartholomew Street, *c.* 1930. Outside the shop (which has now been demolished) are delivery bicycles.

Progress in local delivery vehicles: the fleet of the Woodlands Laundry, of 86 Bartholomew Street, is all lined up and ready to go, early 1930s.

George Hedges' horse-drawn carrier service started in 1917, becoming the Reliance Motor Service of Newbury in 1931. His buses are photographed here in around 1950.

Come shopping in town by bus? The Wharf bus station, April 1947. Newbury &
District Motor Services started services here in 1932.

A Newbury & District single-decker at the Wharf, 22 June 1947. The vehicle is CK
3951, a Leyland Tiger TS2, ex-Ribble Services.

The Wharf, July 1951. By then it was no longer run by Newbury & District Services, having been taken over by Thames Valley Traction the previous year.

A Thames Valley Traction single-decker at the Wharf (looking west) on 19 July 1966. The bus is DMO 655, a rebuilt Bristol L6A.

Market Place, *c.* 1930. It is remembered by an old Newburian as the 'hub of activity, where the real business of a country market town took place' twice a week.

Market day, *c.* 1930. 'Pushing among the stalls . . . there were great bowls of pure lard, chitterlings and faggots and brawn sold by the pork butchers.'

Market Place, photographed from the top of the Town Hall clocktower, around the time of the Second World War. By this time the Corn Exchange was being used for concerts, recitals and shows. Around it are inns: to the left, the Hatchet; to the right, the Queens and further on, the Bear (demolished in 1961 to permit the widening of Bear Lane). Long gone are the days when horses and carts were left in the yards of inns while folk were at the market – the bus and car have taken over.

Market day in Newbury, *c.* 1960. 'The tightly bunched stalls at which you can buy anything from an apple to an armchair, a banana to a box of plants, a loin of pork to a parcel of bed linen . . . the congestion of parked cars, the never-ending procession of traffic crawling through the town . . . the shoppers, the onlookers and the gossipers . . . all these ingredients that go to make up the Market Day scene, and something of the atmosphere too.' (From the *Newbury Weekly News*)

Sporting Days

Newbury's sporting traditions go back a long way. For instance, there was a bowling club at Speenhamland in 1598. Other sporting clubs are relatively recent. The town's football club was founded in 1887 and the rugby club in 1928. Newbury Cricket Club was formed in 1945 by the merging of the Westwood and Great Western cricket clubs. A hockey club was formed in 1952 and amalgamated with the cricket club in 1976. This photograph, from the turn of the century, shows the start of the Guildhall Club walk outside its premises in Bartholomew Street. The participants covered 21 miles, out over Newtown Common to Burghclere, Kingsclere, Headley, Thatcham and back to Newbury. The club opened in 1886 and catered for sports like soccer, cricket, cycling and running. It closed in 1969.

A hockey team at College House School in Bartholomew Street, *c.* 1900. The girls include Gertrude New, Nora Clements, Dolly Bance and Beatrice Pollard.

The Newbury Methodists' Tennis Club, *c.* 1900. The club had a hard court and two grass courts, on land adjacent to Newlands in Porchester Road.

Members of the Westwood Cricket Club, 1930. They are seen in this Hawker photograph with trophies won that season, including the Newbury District Cup and A.J. Maker Challenge Cup. Back row, left to right: T.A.W. Brooks (chairman), E.A. Culley (hon. treasurer), P.L. Davis (hon. sec.), W.G. Hilton. Third row: A.G. Chapman, W.T. Chapman, K.C. Baines, L.T. Wasey (president), A. Hall, F. Longshaw, J.H. Baverstock. Second row: Miss V. Crocker (scorer), J.H. Chapman, E.R. Fifield, J. Crocker (captain), W. Charman, H. Rumball, H. Hillman, H. Allin. Front row: P. Jewell, F.D. Seward, P. Longshaw, J. Small.

Team members of Newbury Cricket Club and the Berkshire Gentlemen, who played one another on the occasion of the Festival of Britain in 1951.

Newbury Cricket Club 1st XI, 1967. The group includes G. Cryer, umpire (standing, right), A. Miller, captain (front row, second from left), M.L. Hutchins, president (front row, centre), and D. Cryer, vice-captain (front row, second from right).

Members of Northcroft Football Club, photographed at the town football ground, 1932. Club players and officials are seen here with trophies won that year, including the Newbury Hospital and Reading Town Junior Cups; they were also champions of the Newbury Junior League. Back row, left to right: Reg Bosley (hon. treasurer), Bill Champ, Bob Davis, Albie Seymour, Ted Jones. Second row: Ted Lawrence (chairman), Harry Pearson, Billy Lock (captain), Wally Bowness, Wally Parsons, Arthur Prisnall (vice-chairman), Perce Anken (trainer). Front row: Warner Taylor, Wally Clinch, Reg Fletcher, George Rosier, Gordy Bowden.

The Newbury Town football team which toured Europe at Easter 1952. They drew 2–2 against French team Maizena Sports at Lille on 13 April.

The Newbury Town football team which beat Hungerford 5–0 in the second round of the Berks and Bucks Senior Cup on 26 February 1955. It was Hungerford's first defeat of the season.

A moment of triumph for Newbury Town Football Club in September 1955. Team captain Dick Slade accepts the Ben Warner Cup from Mrs Desmond Baring. Behind, left, is her father (and donator of the cup) Ben Warner, and in front is her daughter Anne. Also pictured (centre) is Sir William Mount of Wasing Place, then president of the club. Other team members at this date included J. Hartis (goalkeeper), B. Wernham, J. Leach, H.J. Bailey, D. Arthur, E. Vogel, R. Mortimer (who had scored four of the five goals against Hungerford), B. Gabbinni, R. Pasmore and R. West.

Newbury Hockey Club men's team with the winner's trophy from the Southampton Sports Centre six-a-side tournament, 1953. Back row, left to right: Jeremy Goodwin, Hugh Gregor, David Harris. Front row: Bruce Stevens, George Gray, Geoff Vincent.

Fire and Police

A borough fire brigade was established in Newbury in the 1860s but it proved unsatisfactory, so was replaced by a volunteer brigade in 1878. The Second World War brought changes in control of the service: it is now run by Berkshire County Council, which built a new fire station in Hawthorne Road in the 1950s. The Berkshire police constabulary was established in 1856. Newbury's first police station was in Pelican Lane but a new divisional headquarters was built in Mill Lane in 1965. This photograph shows the volunteer fire brigade outside the Town Hall, at the turn of the century. The brigade used two horse-drawn Shand Mason appliances, one bought in 1883 and the other (seen here) in 1900. Its first motorized fire engine was purchased in 1913. The 1883 engine was preserved and auctioned in 1994.

Members of the volunteer fire brigade, *c.* 1900. All were local tradesmen. For example, William Hughes (front, right) was a Northbrook Street caterer. Another member was Edward Martin, who ran a cycle shop in Cheap Street; the brigade captain was Albert Church, who owned Town Mills. The brigade was financed by subscribers, of whom there were 300 in 1911.

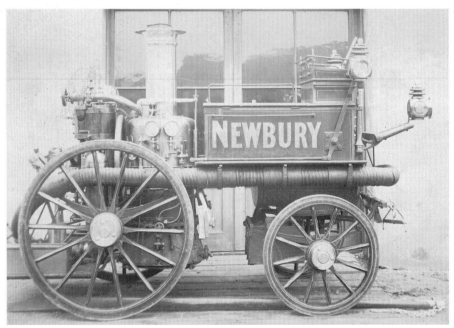

The horse-drawn fire engine of 1883, which was complete with a steam pump and seating for five firemen. Preserved as part of the Hardwick Vehicle Collection, it was auctioned by Sotheby's in 1994.

Members of the volunteer fire brigade, *c.* 1913. The photograph was taken outside the fire station in the Wharf, which the brigade had converted from two old cottages around the turn of the century. The men are seen with the first motorized fire engine, which served for seventeen years. Brigade members include Jim Brindley (back row, left), Bertie Camp (back row, right), Jack Spracklen (middle, third from left), and, in the front row, Frank Lipscombe (left), Ashley Turner (second from left), Teddy Martin (fourth from right), Jack Hassell (second from right) and George 'Smoker' White, stoker on the steam pumps (right).

Personnel of Newbury's national fire service, A3Z section, photographed at the Wharf, *c.* 1944. Company Officer Bert Hooper is seated (front row, centre).

Members of Newbury's wartime brigade with a trailer pump, *c.* 1942. The town brigade had been taken over by the national fire service in August 1941.

A funeral procession in Northbrook Street, 14 March 1941. Three Newbury firemen, Leslie Ford, Albert Miles and Charles Rawlings, had been killed in an air-raid. The fire engine, PG 3076, was the volunteer fire brigade's second motorized vehicle, a Dennis pump escape, purchased in 1930.

The Berkshire Constabulary held an annual inter-divisional sports day, at which a tug o' war contest was a major event. Newbury division often won it and this photograph from about 1923 shows another victorious team. The picture was taken at Pelican Lane, and shows the team with the rope used in the contest and which they 'won' along with the Keyser Cup. A proud Supt. Maunders (civilian dress, left) poses with his men, including P.C. Cecil Gibbons (front, left).

Officers outside the town's original police station in Pelican Lane, where two old cottages were converted for the force around 1878. The Newbury division then included forty-five officers, one mounted. The town's force was under the charge of a superintendent and had constables stationed in the town and surrounding villages. The mounted branch was formed in 1866. The picture was taken for the retirement of Supt. Joseph Maunders, who had served thirty-eight years with the force. He was presented with a gold watch 'as a mark of respect and esteem from the Newbury and Hungerford districts' on 31 March 1925.

A police officer directs traffic around the clocktower, *c.* 1951. The vehicles belong to the USAF, which was returning to Greenham airbase at this time.

Northbrook Street, looking north, *c.* 1951. The Berkshire Constabulary set up an experimental traffic scheme in the town to improve the traffic flow.

Vanishing Newbury

Much of old Newbury has changed or disappeared as a result of highway and redevelopment schemes. Newbury's role as a road hub required the construction of a ring road to ease town-centre traffic congestion. Consequently an east–west relief road opened in 1959 and a north–south one followed in 1965. This photograph shows the London Road (looking east) at its junction with the east–west relief road (and Shaw Crescent), *c.* 1962. At this time the north–south relief road was under construction, along with a new roundabout. This was named after the Robin Hood pub (upper right), and necessitated the demolition of the Greyhound pub (centre). To the right of the picture, land has been cleared to make way for the new road leading south from the roundabout.

The relief road had to cross the River Kennet alongside Victoria Park, for which purpose a modern road bridge had to be erected over the waterway.

This new bridge was constructed from pre-cast concrete sections, which were delivered to the riverside site by road vehicles, as shown here, in 1964.

To support the bridge, 60 ft pier foundations were sunk into the riverbed, with divers working at the same depth. The centre arch spanned 107 ft of waterway.

Work on the new bridge started just before Christmas 1963. It was finally opened to road traffic on the afternoon of Monday 13 September 1965.

Further south the road crossed the railway and connected with Cheap Street, shown here (looking north). The Railway Hotel has now been demolished.

The same location, looking south. The access road to the station is off to the right. A new 140 ft span overbridge was erected to carry the relief road over the railway.

Gone but not forgotten: the fondly remembered Axe & Compass pub, located in Cheap Street by the entrance to the railway goods yard. The pub was demolished in about 1964 to make way for the relief road.

This photograph (looking north) shows the new dual carriageway relief road where it cut through the edge of Greenham House gardens. The house stands exposed on the far side of what became the new A34 in 1965.

Shown here and on the following four pages are properties which have been demolished. The eight houses in Brixton Rise (off Cheap Street), photographed in 1961, were pulled down to make way for the new relief road.

These houses in Market Street, seen here in May 1961, were demolished for town centre redevelopment in about 1965. Note the election posters in the windows.

Trafalgar Place (off Bartholomew Street), *c.* 1960. This terrace had no back gardens but there were earth closets in the front gardens.

Pelican Terrace (off Pelican Lane), October 1961. Westbourne Terrace (left) still stands.

The passageway leading into Crown Court from Bartholomew Street, *c.* 1960.

Crown Court, *c.* 1960. There were only three tall houses here.

The terrace of houses in St John's View (off Bartholomew Street), July 1960.

Town-centre houses in New Square (off Bartholomew Street), *c.* 1960.

Brixton Rise (off Cheap Street), looking across to the relief road, 1961.

Nos 30–2 King's Road, looking north, 1959. These houses were demolished to make way for the relief road.

Jack Street (an alleyway off Northbrook Street), 1961. The site is now a car park.

Gilders Square (off Oxford Street), leading to the Pelican theatre, *c.* 1960.

A wintry scene in Bedford Place (leading off Bartholomew Street), 1962. These one-up, one-down properties were demolished in about 1963.

The rear of Bedford Place and New Square, looking north to Inch's Yard, *c.* 1961. The new Council office complex was built here in 1982.

SECTION NINE

Highway

Newbury's streets have been transformed by the growth in motor traffic since the turn of the century. In May 1900 the Earl of Carnarvon – one of the first car owners in the locality – was summoned at Newbury Police Court. P.C. Pounds reported that he was in Bartholomew Street when the earl drove by at an excessive speed: 'The car went by like a flash of lightning. . . . I should say it was travelling from 20 to 25 miles an hour.' The case was dismissed, but it was a sign of things to come. Above, looking north from outside Bridge House, *c.* 1900. Before the town's doctor sold his gig and the local farmers replaced their market carts, the various forms of horse-drawn transport had Newbury's streets to themselves.

Northbrook Street, looking south from outside Staple's the confectioner, when horse power reigned supreme, around the turn of the century.

Bartholomew Street, looking north, c. 1914. Bicycles, and the much safer tricycle, are much in evidence; E.C. Wheeler's cycle shop is on the corner.

A broad view of Northbrook Street, looking north at about the time of the First World War. Change is in the air, as a pony and trap is overtaken by a car. The car appears to be a model 40/50 Hotchkiss: these elegant vehicles were of American design and French manufacture, but the marque was available in England through an agent. This model was introduced in 1913 for a price of £890, at a time when the wealthier middle class was forsaking horse power in favour of the more popular automobile.

Northbrook Street, looking north from outside Liddiard's the butcher, late 1920s. The motor car has well and truly arrived on Newbury's streets.

Bartholomew Street, looking north from outside the Savings Bank, 1920s. All the cars are heading south; in today's one-way system vehicles travel in the opposite direction.

Market Place, June 1928. To the left are the premises of Messrs Edwards and Godding, ironmongers, gas and electrical engineers. Behind Queen Victoria's statue are the premises of Beynon's, a drapery business established in 1827. Note the freshly marked-out parking spaces – these were the result of a by-law enacted earlier in 1928 which permitted a maximum wait of forty-five minutes, but no parking was allowed on Thursdays, Saturdays or at night. Parking in Market Place was a controversial issue in Newbury in 1928, according to the *Newbury Weekly News*.

The Broadway, 1950s. Directional, keep-left and roundabout signs have appeared to regulate the traffic flow.

Commercial vehicles in Bartholomew Street, 1950s. The van parked on the left belongs to Newbury Model Bakeries of 22 Bartholomew Street.

The view into Market Place from Cheap Street, *c.* 1950. The motor car has taken over the streets completely, although the proliferation of traffic-lights, bollards, islands and yellow lines of today is not yet apparent.

Bartholomew Street, looking north, 1950s. The eighteenth-century red-brick house on the left still stands but Herborough House (seen here as Nias Garage) was demolished to make way for the Kennet Centre. A cyclist makes his way among the cars; the number of private cars in Britain rose from 8,465 in 1904 to 1,944,394 by 1938. That year, to cope with the exceptionally heavy traffic over the bank holiday weekend, the chief constable decreed that Bartholomew Street should temporarily become one-way.

Market Place, looking north, 1950s. On the left, the shoe shop still stands, as it has done for centuries; inscribed on its ornamental triple gable is the date 1679. On the right, the square-fronted almshouse of Kimber's charity (founded in 1795) is now gone, having been demolished in the 1960s. For some two hundred years, until the Second World War, the town's Michaelmas Fair was held in Market Place each October. The first postwar fair caused so much traffic congestion here that it had to be transferred to the Northcroft from 1946.

Northbrook Street, looking south, 1950s. There are vehicles as far as the eye can see. In August 1954 a census taken by Newbury Corporation showed the full extent of the problem. Six enumerators were employed from 8 a.m. to 8 p.m. on a Friday and a Saturday, and the numbers of cars counted on the Saturday afternoon were as follows: between 12 p.m. and 1 p.m. there were 531 cars; between 1 p.m. and 2 p.m., 535 cars; between 2 p.m. and 3 p.m., 548 cars; between 3 p.m. and 4 p.m., 551 cars; between 4 p.m. and 5 p.m., 526 cars; and between 5 p.m. and 6 p.m., 590 cars.

A motorist's-eye view of the same congested street, with traffic bumper to bumper. No wonder Newbury Corporation was pressing the Ministry of Transport for a by-pass round the town. Their census recorded that a total of 41,444 vehicles passed the Broadway clocktower, at a rate of 1,200 an hour at peak times, in two twelve-hour periods on a Friday and Saturday. A breakdown of the total was as follows: private cars, 23,492; motorcycles and combinations, 3,000; buses and coaches, 1,734; light goods vehicles, 2,808; heavy goods vehicles, 3,270 (including six traction engines); pedal cycles, 6,933.

Northbrook Street, looking north, *c.* 1960. It is sobering to remember that this street constituted part of the Winchester–Preston trunk road until 1965. The Buchanan Report, 'Traffic in Towns' (1963), made Newbury its first case study and began by examining periods of heavy traffic flow. The experts concluded: 'Newbury's traffic problems can only be solved by drastic and expensive measures on a scale hitherto unexpected in a town of its size.' Otherwise, they predicted, the town's 'existing road system cannot possibly carry the enormously increased loads of the next 50 years'. Prophetic words indeed.

Railway

The railway first came to Newbury in 1847 in the form of a branch of the GWR's main line, starting at Reading and ending at Hungerford. Various extensions over the years resulted in this line becoming the GWR's direct route to the West Country by 1906. Newbury became a junction station in 1882, with the opening of a line to Didcot (extended to Southampton by 1891). Another branch from Newbury to Lambourn was opened in 1898. Newbury's original station was a modest affair with an overall roof accommodating a double track. When the line became the direct route to the West Country the station was rebuilt and enlarged, with quadruple tracks and bays for local services. This work was completed in May 1910. The station is shown here during a one-day strike in 1962.

The railway station, looking east, before it was rebuilt, *c.* 1908. The overall roof is still in existence; the tall structure on the left is a water tank.

The station, looking east, after it was rebuilt, *c.* 1915. There are four through lines, with bays for local trains. Note the coaching stock in the siding.

The station, looking west, 1930s. A 'Duke' class engine waits, with a short local train, at one of the platforms. Note the array of advertisements on the station approach road.

No. 6320 arrives at Newbury station, passing under the (old) road bridge, *c.* 1960. Though only a modest mixed traffic locomotive, it carries an express lamp indication.

The interior of Newbury East Junction signal-box, with signalman James Humphrey on duty *c*. 1957. The box was demolished in about 1978.

The goods yard at the east end of Newbury station and the old Victorian goods shed, 1948. This fine building was demolished in about 1978.

A splendid photograph of the interior of Newbury's goods shed, from a glass plate negative of about 1904. Seven of the staff are shown here; two shunters (with poles), two goods porters and three clerks (just inside the office door). The merchandise being handled includes wooden boxes of Sunlight Soap and packing cases marked W.D. & H.O. Wills, presumably containing cigarettes. Heavy goods were transferred from road to rail (and vice versa) by means of the crane. When the goods shed was demolished, the crane was salvaged and re-erected at Newbury Wharf, where a similar device once stood.

A general view of the main line west of Newbury station, near Enborne Junction, which was the scene of an accident (below and opposite) in 1944, when the railways were operating under difficult wartime conditions.

On the morning of Friday 25 August a goods train overran a siding, ploughed into the ballast at its end, and caused a pile-up, obstructing the main line.

The mishap partly derailed the goods train; the engine and six of the wagons came off the tracks. Fortunately, no one was injured in the accident.

Breakdown gangs had a single line service open from Newbury to Enborne within two hours, and normal main line service was restored by 6.30 p.m.

'The train now floating at platform four . . .'. An unseasonal view of Newbury station, with the line looking more like a river, during a downpour in August 1959.

A snow scene in the goods yard (seen here with a diesel loco), during the winter of 1962/3. The view is from Railway Road across to Gordon Road.

The full complement of staff at Newbury station, including passenger office, goods office and permanent way employees, *c.* 1950. Back row, left to right: Alf Wells, Jack Miller. Third row: Peter Timpson, Bert Dew, Jack Shaw, Dick Tungate, Bill Davies, Les Barden, Bob Stephenson, Bill Hazell. Second row: -?- (standing, back), Alec McGovern, Chris Clements, Brian Merchant, Reg Harry (standing, front), John Allen, Fred Crockett, Bill Best, Fred Ginger, Inspector Jeremy, Phil Knapp, Bill Winter, Frank Hammond, Steve Stacey, Bob Aldridge, Rene Winter, Lionel Preseck. Front row: Joan Bayton, Chris Allen, Mrs Cinderbury, Barbara Paget, John F. Snow (stationmaster), Frank Cyrils, Elsie Smith, Gwen Sheriff, Betty Smallbones, Sheila Stacey.

Three of the Newbury goods staff photographed in the yard, 7 March 1948. From left to right: shunters John Humphrey, Fred Richens, Bill Guy. The latter's father, Bill Guy snr, had also been a shunter at Newbury goods yard. In all, nine shunters and a foreman were employed at the yard, which was 'open all hours' – it only closed on Sunday nights. Newbury goods yard finally ceased to function as such in the mid-seventies. The small brick shunters' cabin (right) still stands today in what remains of the goods yard.

SECTION ELEVEN

Waterway

The Canal. Newbury.
N.º 5132

As the town of Newbury developed, the River Kennet became important as the lifeblood of its transport and trade. From 1723 the river was made navigable through to Reading, and became known as the Kennet Navigation. It was extended cross country to Bath (and thence to Bristol) as the Kennet & Avon Canal from 1810. However, the canal went into decline after the arrival of the railway and in 1852 the K&A sold out to the GWR. This photograph shows the canal above Newbury Lock, *c.* 1920. There are three wide boats (over 7 ft) in view. The boat on the left may be *Betty*, belonging to Dolton's, while the one in the centre, right, is *Defiance*, one of Ferris's boats, looking rather the worse for wear!

A postcard view of the canal bend above the wharf, *c.* 1900. Just to the right of centre is the Presbyterian chapel, which was built in 1697 and demolished in the 1950s.

Newbury Lock early this century. Built in 1796, it was a broad lock with a brick lock chamber. The lock cottage (right) was burned down in October 1989.

The wharf at West Mills, looking east, *c.* 1865. By this date the K & A canal had been in GWR ownership for several years and had lost much of its traffic to the railway. Nevertheless, a narrow barge, constructed for use on the narrow canals, waits to unload its cargo of coal at the wharf. Visible in the background is the chimney of the old West Mills Brewery. The original Town Mill building (left) was burned down but was re-erected in 1892. It was purchased by Hovis in 1921, then by Dolton's in 1956, but was demolished to make way for redevelopment in 1972.

Ham Mills, at the confluence of the Rivers Kennet and Lambourn, on the eastern fringe of Newbury, c. 1912. There were actually two flour mills here.

A view of the canal near Ham Mill swingbridge, looking east, c. 1913. The moored wide boat probably belongs to the Ferris family, who operated a few boats on the canal.

West Mills, June 1928. This part of Newbury has long been associated with the milling industry. Corn grinding, cloth fulling and paper making have been carried on here at different times. Among the premises along the road (right) at this date were those of Messrs Stuart, the dairymen who operated the A1 Dairies from West Mills House. West Mills (left) was purchased by Hovis in 1921 but was damaged by a fire in 1965 and demolished in 1972. Flats were then built on the site.

The canal above Newbury Lock, 1928. *Defiance* lay derelict here for over half a century, and was only removed when Town Mill was redeveloped.

Looking downstream to Newbury Bridge, *c.* 1930. This was once triple arched, but the buildings around it encroached upon the outer arches, leaving only the centre arch visible.

A close-up of the bridge, *c.* 1930. Walter Money wrote: 'The old wooden bridge, which for centuries spanned the swift-flowing Kennet at Newbury, adorned with timber-framed houses over-hanging the river on either side like one continuous street, was taken down in 1769, and the first stone of the present structure was laid 28th July in that year.' Built by Mr James Clarke, it took three years to erect and cost over £700.

A wintry scene at West Mills, 25 February 1950. The motor boat *Columba* is waiting to unload its cargo of 27 tons of salt, which it has brought from Middlewich, Cheshire. Its route was via the Trent & Mersey, Coventry, Oxford and Kennet & Avon canals. This was the first fully loaded working boat to come up the K&A for twenty-five years. Before this, the last working boats to do so was a pair of narrow boats bringing grain to Newbury for Messrs Hovis in 1925. It is interesting to compare this photograph of West Mills with the one on page 119, taken ninety years earlier.

Paddling through the top gate at Newbury Lock, 1957. Note the lock cottage, then still extant, and, in the background, the old Temperance Hall in Northcroft Lane.

A view of the canal, looking east, from above Newbury Lock, *c*. 1960. By this date pleasure craft had taken over from working boats on the canal.

A distant view of Newbury, looking west along the canal towards the town centre, *c.* 1910. Landmarks which can be identified include the Corn Exchange, Town Hall, parish church and Newbury Wharf.

Acknowledgements

Sincere thanks are due to all those individuals and organizations who contributed materials used in the compilation of this book. I am deeply indebted to them for loaning cherished photographs for copying, and for supplying information for captions. Responsibility for any errors that may have inadvertently occurred in the background research rests with me alone. The pictorial record of Newbury in days gone by has been enriched in variety and scope by contributions from the following:

Mr B. Bowness • Mr R. Brown • Revd D.R. Bunney • Mr B. Burge
Mrs R. Burge • Mr I. Coulson • Mrs D. Delahunty • Miss J. Gibbons
Mr J.C. Gillham • Mr J. Gould • Mr C.C. Hall • Mrs M. Hassell
Revd R. Herrington • Mrs J. Hughes • Mr J. Humphrey • Mrs C. Isaacs
Mrs J. Jackson • Mrs J. Kennedy • Mrs D. Milner • Mrs J. Money
Mr R. Slade • Mr E.A. Stacey • Mrs J. Strong • Mr A.A. Wells
Lens of Sutton • Newbury Cricket Club • Newbury Hockey Club
Newbury Reference Library • Newbury United Reformed Church
Newbury Weekly News • Thames Valley Police

To order any of these titles please telephone Littlehampton Book Services on 01903 721596